The Delivered
MARRIAGE
DEVOTIONAL

Dedicated to The Core Couples , who we absolutely love and adore.

You are the reason we wrote this and we pray it blesses you mightlity.

WE NEED DELIVERANCE?

Psalm 34:17-19 (NIV)
"The righteous cry out, and the Lord hears them; he delivers them from all their troubles. The Lord is close to the brokenhearted and saves those who are crushed in spirit. The righteous person may have many troubles, but the Lord delivers him from them all."

Dear married couple, have you ever wondered if your marriage needs deliverance? Do you find yourselves facing challenges that seem insurmountable? Take heart, for you are not alone. Many couples have walked this path, and God's Word assures us that He is our deliverer.

Marriage is a beautiful union designed by God, but it is not immune to the trials and tribulations of life. We live in a fallen world, surrounded by spiritual warfare that seeks to steal, kill, and destroy (John 10:10). The enemy will attempt to sow seeds of discord, resentment, and division within your marriage. But as believers in Christ, we have the power to overcome through His deliverance.

Deliverance in a marriage begins by recognizing the need for it. It requires humility and a willingness to confront the areas in which the enemy may have gained a foothold. It is not a sign of weakness to admit that your marriage needs deliverance; rather, it is an act of faith and trust in God's transforming power.

Identify the strongholds that may be hindering your relationship. These can include unforgiveness, bitterness, pride, or selfishness. Reflect on your actions and attitudes, and ask the Holy Spirit to reveal any areas that need His healing touch.

Seek God's presence through prayer. Together as a couple, bring your concerns, burdens, and struggles before the Lord. Pour out your hearts to Him, for He is near to the brokenhearted and saves those who are crushed in spirit (Psalm 34:18). Pray for His deliverance, wisdom, and guidance to navigate the challenges you face.

Claim the promises of God's Word. Meditate on scriptures that declare His faithfulness and power to deliver. Scripture such as Psalm 34:17-19 reminds us that when the righteous cry out, the Lord hears and delivers them from all their troubles. Hold on to these promises and let them strengthen your faith.

COUPLES PRAYER:

Heavenly Father, we come before You as a married couple in need of Your deliverance. We acknowledge the challenges we face and the areas in our hearts and relationship that need Your healing touch. We ask for Your forgiveness for any unforgiveness, bitterness, or selfishness that may have crept in. Lord, we invite Your Holy Spirit to reign in our marriage, to guide us, and to help us grow in love and unity. We declare that You are our deliverer, and we trust in Your faithfulness to bring restoration and healing. In Jesus' name, Amen.

REFLECTION:

Take a moment to reflect on the areas in your marriage that may need deliverance. Write them down and bring them before the Lord in prayer. Surrender them to Him, trusting in His power to bring healing and restoration. As you continue on this journey, remember that deliverance is a process, requiring faith, perseverance, and a deep reliance on God. Seek His face daily, and be open to His transforming work in your lives and marriage. Trust in His promises, and know that He is with you every step of the way.

DELIVERANCE DECREES
DESTROYING STRONGHOLDS

As Believers we have the authority to speak forth decrees that break the power of strongholds in our lives. By declaring these words out loud, we align ourselves with the truth of God's Word and invite His deliverance into our marriage.

Decree:
I break every stronghold of discord, strife, bitterness, and unforgiveness that might attack my marriage. I decree that these strongholds are uprooted and cast out in the name of Jesus. According to 2 Corinthians 10:4, "For the weapons of our warfare are not carnal, but mighty in God for pulling down strongholdst.

Renunciations:
We renounce any spirit of division, strife, and conflict in my marriage. I choose to embrace unity, understanding, and love. I declare that our relationship is built on the foundation of Christ, who calls us to live in harmony with one another.

We renounce any fear and insecurity that have taken root in our hearts regarding our marriage. We will not allow fear of failure, rejection, or inadequacy to dictate our actions. Instead, We choose to embrace the perfect love of God that casts out all fear and to trust in His plan for our union.

We renounce the brokenness and past wounds that have affected our marriage. We choose to forgive each other for past mistakes, and we commit to healing and restoration. We declare that our marriage is made new in Christ, and we will walk forward in faith and hope together.

We renounce any shame and guilt that have weighed down our hearts and hindered our relationship with each other. We acknowledge that we are forgiven in Christ, and we choose to release these burdens. We commit to walking in the light of His grace and extending that same grace to each other.

WIFE'S
thoughts

HUSBAND'S
thoughts

LET'S START WITH FORGIVENESS

WRITTEN BY STEPHEN WEAVER

Ephesians 4:32 (NIV)
"Be kind and compassionate to one another, forgiving each other, just as in Christ God forgave you."

Dear married couple, in our journey towards deliverance in our marriages, we must begin with forgiveness. Forgiveness is a powerful tool that releases us from the bondage of resentment, bitterness, and hurt. It is an important step towards having true deliverance and restoration in our relationship.

In marriage, we are two imperfect people, can I get an Amen on that? We are prone to making mistakes and hurting one another. The build up of hurts and offenses can create strongholds that hinder the free flow of love and unity. But listen my friends, forgiveness breaks the chains and opens the door for God's healing and deliverance to take place.

Forgiveness does not mean dismissing or minimizing the pain caused by our spouse's actions. It is a choice to release the burden of anger, resentment, and the desire for revenge. It is an act of surrendering our right to hold on to the offenses and entrusting justice into God's hands. You have to let that unforgiveness go!

Reflect on your own heart and ask yourself, "Am I holding on to unforgiveness towards my spouse?" Allow the Holy Spirit to reveal any areas where forgiveness is needed. Remember, forgiveness is not a one-time event but a continuous process. It may involve forgiving past hurts, as well as extending forgiveness in the present and future.

God's Word instructs us to be kind and compassionate to one another, forgiving each other, just as in Christ God forgave us (Ephesians 4:32). We are called to imitate Christ's forgiveness towards us. When we understand the depth of God's forgiveness, we realize that we, too, are called to extend that forgiveness to our spouse. The more you do it, the easier it gets.

COUPLES PRAYER:

Heavenly Father, we come before You as a couple in need of your grace and forgiveness. We acknowledge the hurts and offenses that have accumulated between us. Today, we choose to release the burden of unforgiveness and lay down our right to hold on to the pain. We ask for Your help to forgive one another, just as You have forgiven us. Fill our hearts with Your love, compassion, and understanding. May forgiveness pave the way for deliverance and restoration in our marriage. In Jesus' name, Amen.

REFLECTION:

Take a moment to reflect on any areas of unforgiveness in your marriage. Write down the hurts and offenses that have been weighing you down. Surrender them to God in prayer, asking for His help to release forgiveness and embrace the freedom it brings. Remember that forgiveness is a journey, and it may take time and intentional effort. Trust in God's healing power and His ability to transform your hearts and marriage through forgiveness.

As you embark on this path of forgiveness, be patient with one another and yourselves. Seek God's guidance and wisdom as you navigate the process. Allow His love and grace to flow through you, extending forgiveness as He has forgiven you. Embrace the freedom and restoration that forgiveness brings, knowing that it is a vital step towards experiencing deliverance in your marriage.

DELIVERANCE DECREES

BREAKING THE SPIRIT OF UNFORGIVENESS AND BITTERNESS

As Believers we have the authority to speak forth decrees that break the power of unforgiveness and bitterness in our lives. By declaring these words out loud, we align ourselves with the truth of God's Word and invite His deliverance into our marriage.

Decree:

In the name of Jesus, we decree that unforgiveness and bitterness have no place in our hearts and marriage. We declare that we are vessels of love, grace, and forgiveness. We choose to release all offenses and hurts, surrendering them to the Lord. Our marriage is a sanctuary of forgiveness and healing, reflecting the character of Christ.

Renunciations:

We renounce the spirit of unforgiveness and bitterness that has taken root in our hearts. We refuse to be bound by its destructive power any longer. By the authority given to us in Christ, we break every chain of unforgiveness and bitterness in our lives.

We renounce the lies of the enemy that tell us we cannot forgive or that we are justified in holding on to bitterness. We reject these lies and choose to embrace the truth of God's Word, which calls us to forgive as we have been forgiven.

We renounce the cycle of resentment and revenge. We refuse to perpetuate a spirit of unforgiveness and bitterness in our marriage. Instead, we choose to respond with love, compassion, and a willingness to reconcile.

We renounce any agreements we have made with the spirit of unforgiveness and bitterness. We break those agreements and declare that we are now aligned with the truth of God's Word, which calls us to forgive and love one another deeply.

We renounce any generational patterns of unforgiveness and bitterness that have influenced our lives and marriage. By the blood of Jesus, we break these generational chains and declare a new legacy of forgiveness and grace.

WIFE'S
thoughts

HUSBAND'S
thoughts

DELIVERANCE THROUGH HUMILITY

WRITTEN BY JENNY WEAVER

James 4:10 (NIV) - "Humble yourselves before the Lord, and he will lift you up."

Dear couple on the journey of marriage and deliverance, humility is a cornerstone for God's transformative work in our lives and relationships. In the a marriage, humility plays a vital role in fostering understanding, forgiveness, and unity.

Humility in marriage means setting aside pride and self-centeredness to prioritize your spouse's needs, feelings, and well-being. It involves listening with an open heart, admitting faults, and being willing to seek reconciliation. Guess what? You're not always right! I know that's a shock to many of you but it's true.
When both partners walk in humility, they create a fertile ground for God's grace to bring healing and deliverance.

Scripture is clear about the importance of humility. James 4:10 reminds us to "Humble yourselves before the Lord, and he will lift you up." When we humble ourselves before God, acknowledging our dependence on Him and our need for His guidance, He exalts us in His perfect timing. In your marriage this humility extends to your spouse, as we honor them, serve them, and seek their good above our own. Ask yourself, "Am i walking in humility in this marriage?"

Walking in humility requires vulnerability and transparency. It involves confessing our mistakes, asking for forgiveness, and extending grace to one another. When conflicts arise, humility softens hearts, creates understanding, and paves the way for reconciliation. It is a posture that reflects the love and humility of Christ, who humbled Himself to the point of death on the cross for our sake.

Here's the bottom line... demons hold on to a person where there is pride. You want to maintain a strong Holy Ghost filled loving marriage without constant attacks and open doors to the demonic? Then you must start today with walking in humility.

Old habits of having to be right, thinking you're better than your spouse must end today.

COUPLES PRAYER:

Heavenly Father, we come before You humbly, recognizing our need for Your wisdom and grace in our marriage. Teach us to walk in humility towards one another, putting aside pride and self-interest. Help us to listen with compassion, speak with kindness, and serve one another with love. May our marriage be a reflection of Your humility and grace. We invite Your presence to lead us on the path of deliverance and transformation. In Jesus' name, Amen.

REFLECTION:

Take a moment to reflect on your attitudes and actions towards your spouse. Are there areas where pride or self-centeredness have hindered your relationship? Ask God to reveal any areas where humility is needed and pray for the strength to walk in humility towards your spouse. Remember that humility is not a sign of weakness but a mark of strength and love in a marriage.

As you embrace humility in your marriage, trust in God's promise to lift you up. Surrender your pride, fears, and insecurities to Him, knowing that He will exalt your marriage and bring healing and deliverance as you humble yourselves before Him and each other. Embrace the beauty of humility in marriage and watch how God transforms your relationship for His glory.

DELIVERANCE DECREES

BREAKING THE SPIRIT OF UNFORGIVENESS AND BITTERNESS

As spirit-filled Christian couples, we have the authority to speak forth decrees and renunciations that break the power of pride and invite the spirit of humility into our lives and marriage. Let us declare these words out loud, aligning ourselves with God's truth and inviting His transformative work:

Decree:
In the name of Jesus, we decree that pride has no place in our hearts, minds, or marriage. We declare that we choose humility as a guiding principle in our relationship. We lay down our pride before the Lord and invite His spirit of humility to reign in our lives and marriage.

Renunciations:
We renounce the spirit of pride that exalts itself above God and others. We reject the lies of self-sufficiency, arrogance, and self-centeredness. By the authority given to us in Christ, we break every stronghold of pride in our lives and marriage.

We renounce the masks of perfectionism and superiority that pride often wears. We refuse to portray ourselves as flawless or better than others. Instead, we choose authenticity, vulnerability, and a humble posture before God and each other.

We renounce the fear of vulnerability and the need to always be right. We let go of the need to defend ourselves and our egos. Instead, we embrace the humility that comes from admitting our weaknesses, seeking forgiveness, and growing in grace.

We renounce any agreements we have made with the spirit of pride, knowingly or unknowingly. We break those agreements and declare that we are now aligned with God's truth, which calls us to walk humbly, love mercy, and act justly.

WIFE'S
thoughts

HUSBAND'S
thoughts

FASTING FOR FREEDOM

WRITTEN BY JENNY WEAVER

Matthew 17:21 (NIV) - "But this kind does not go out except by prayer and fasting."

Dar kingdom couple seeking deliverance, fasting and prayer hold immense power in breaking strongholds and ushering in freedom in your marriage. Fasting is a spiritual discipline that involves abstaining from food or certain luxuries for a period of time to seek God wholeheartedly. When combined with prayer, fasting becomes a potent tool for spiritual breakthrough and deliverance.

Let's look at your marriage, fasting as a couple can deepen your spiritual intimacy, align your hearts with God's will, and break chains of bondage that hinder your relationship. Fasting together not only strengthens your unity but also amplifies your prayers, creating a focused and fervent atmosphere for God to work in your marriage. Doesn't that sound amazing?!

The Bible teaches us about the significance of fasting and prayer in seeking deliverance. In Matthew 17:21, Jesus tells His disciples that certain kinds of spiritual strongholds can only be overcome through prayer and fasting. By engaging in these practices, we demonstrate our reliance on God's power to bring about transformation and deliverance in our lives and marriages.

Fasting is more than just abstaining from food; it is a posture of humility, surrender, and dependence on God. When couples fast together, they demonstrate their unity in seeking God's intervention and deliverance. As you sacrifice the comfort of food, you open yourselves up to receive God's guidance, healing, and breakthrough in areas where deliverance is needed.

If there are certain things in your marriage that just can't seem to get better, or if one or both of you are struggling with sin cycles , strongholds or demonic patterns then I highly recommend starting as fast as soon as you can.

Start by asking the Lord how He wants you to go about it. Its ok to start with a day as well, you'll be surprised what 24 hours of fasting together as a couple will produce in your lives.

COUPLES PRAYER:

Lord Jesus, we come before You in humility, recognizing our need for deliverance in our marriage. As we embark on this journey of fasting and prayer, we ask for Your presence to be magnified in our midst. Grant us the strength and discipline to fast with a purpose, seeking Your face earnestly. May our prayers rise as a sweet fragrance before Your throne, bringing about deliverance, healing, and restoration in our marriage. In Jesus' name, Amen.

REFLECTION:

Consider setting aside a day or a specific time to fast and pray together as a couple. Seek God's guidance on areas in your marriage where deliverance is needed. Reflect on any strongholds, patterns, or struggles that you desire God to break and surrender them to Him in prayer.

As you fast for freedom, remember that God sees your sacrifice and hears your prayers. Trust in His faithfulness to bring deliverance and transformation in your marriage as you seek Him wholeheartedly through fasting and prayer. Embrace this time of seeking God's face together, knowing that He is the ultimate deliverer and healer in your lives and relationship.

DELIVERANCE DECREES

BREAKING THE SPIRIT OF UNFORGIVENESS AND BITTERNESS

As Believers we have the authority to speak forth decrees that break the power of unforgiveness and bitterness in our lives. By declaring these words out loud, we align ourselves with the truth of God's Word and invite His deliverance into our marriage.

Decree:

In the name of Jesus, we decree that unforgiveness and bitterness have no place in our hearts and marriage. We declare that we are vessels of love, grace, and forgiveness. We choose to release all offenses and hurts, surrendering them to the Lord. Our marriage is a sanctuary of forgiveness and healing, reflecting the character of Christ.

Renunciations:

We renounce the spirit of unforgiveness and bitterness that has taken root in our hearts. We refuse to be bound by its destructive power any longer. By the authority given to us in Christ, we break every chain of unforgiveness and bitterness in our lives.

We renounce the lies of the enemy that tell us we cannot forgive or that we are justified in holding on to bitterness. We reject these lies and choose to embrace the truth of God's Word, which calls us to forgive as we have been forgiven.

We renounce the cycle of resentment and revenge. We refuse to perpetuate a spirit of unforgiveness and bitterness in our marriage. Instead, we choose to respond with love, compassion, and a willingness to reconcile.

We renounce any agreements we have made with the spirit of unforgiveness and bitterness. We break those agreements and declare that we are now aligned with the truth of God's Word, which calls us to forgive and love one another deeply.

We renounce any generational patterns of unforgiveness and bitterness that have influenced our lives and marriage. By the blood of Jesus, we break these generational chains and declare a new legacy of forgiveness and grace.

WIFE'S
thoughts

HUSBAND'S
thoughts

REDEMPTION FROM THE DEPTHS

WRITTEN BY JASON & KENDRA KEENAN

Romans 3:4 (NIV)
"And all are justified freely by his grace through the redemption that came by Christ Jesus."

D ear married couples we want to share with you about how the redemptive love of God transformed our marriage. A Godly marriage was always important to the both of us, but we didn't know how to quite prepare for it. We were both still stubborn, in the world, dabbling in worldly pleasures, but visiting church and calling ourselves Christians by title and affiliation. We knew we loved God, but we really didn't understand true relationship and surrender to him.

The Lord's plan of redemption began to unfold before us when we both overcame the spirit of premature death by His grace alone! What was interesting was this would all take place during wedding planning: the enemy had an assignment on our lives. He would try to steal, kill, and destroy us by any means necessary. He knew this marriage was different. There was a timetable on his agenda he would strike us both while wedding planning so this wedding wouldn't happen, but God said different. His plan of redemptive love was to save us.

It all began while trying to plan our wedding. Prior to this we had our problems, like everyone else, but it was something about the covenant of marriage that was detestable to the enemy. It would bring us out of fornication and our obedience would honor God, it would put us out of covenant with him and into alignment with God.

We overcame death on several occasions. The enemy studied us and knew when to strike. He had a plan to take us out at different times as we prepared to be married.

My wife would lay ill in a hospital bed fighting to live. My wife became septic stage 2 and was on the verge of death and needed several blood transfusions and a strand of several antibiotics to help her heal. Even at the hospital every antibiotic she became allergic to. The enemy did not want her to live he wanted to take her life. She wasn't allergic to anything, but ended up being allergic to all antibiotics at the time. BUT GOD! After much prayer from friends and family, several blood transfusions and a cocktail strain of antibiotics the Lord cleansed her blood and prepared an antibiotic cocktail specifically for her body, Jesus Christ healed her! He cleansed her with His blood and overnight it was as if a LIGHT SWITCH was turned on she was made well.

In the weeks before we were to be married the enemy attacked again and my husband had a stroke, with a blood pressure of 265/196. The doctors said he should have been dead. He lost use of his entire right side including his right eye.

While my husband cried out to the Lord in his weakest moments, I'd later find out during that time I was also interceding in prayer for him. There is so much power in prayer! On his 3rd day in the hospital the Lord answered him and his leg moved involuntarily after being told he needed intense physical therapy to gain mobility they had assigned a walker to him and he was able to stand later that day! He took steps, on day 5. I witnessed him walk up 15 steps in order to be released ,doctors informed us there was zero damage or blockages in his body and couldn't explain it scientifically.

The hand of God was on my husband and in 12 weeks he walked down the aisle with no walker or cane and we danced our first dance as man and wife. We honored God with our obedience. We were now ready to live out a delivered and restored marriage.

COUPLES PRAYER:

Father, we pray for open communication, understanding, and empathy between each other. May our love and grace be the foundation of our marriage, and may we seek to honor and respect each other in all things. Grant us the faith to believe that through your power, all things are possible, and that even in the midst of brokenness, you can bring about redemption and restoration. We ask for your blessing upon our union and trust that you will lead us to a place of wholeness and joy in our marriage. In Jesus name, Amen.

REFLECTION:

How did the accounts of restoration and physical healing within their marriage resonate with you? Reflect on the transformative power of faith, love, and perseverance within a marriage. There's nothing too hard for God. He can redem your relationship and help you to have resilience of love and hope for restoration in your marriage.

Additionally, ponder the significance of perseverance, faith, and surrender in allowing for God's miraculous work within our lives and relationships.

DELIVERANCE DECREES
BREAKING THE SPIRIT OF DIVISION

As Believers we have the authority to speak forth decrees that break the power of division in our lives and families. By declaring these words out loud, we align ourselves with the truth of God's Word and invite His deliverance into our marriage.

Decree:

In the name of Jesus we decree that our marriage is redeemed by the precious blood of Jesus. We renounce every negative word, lie, and incident that has tried to separate us. We destroy the spirit of division. We proclaim that we are one flesh, united by God's design, and no weapon formed against us shall prosper.

Renunciations:

We renounce the pain of our past and the bitterness that may have taken root in our hearts. We forgive each other completely, letting go of old grievances and trusting in God's power to heal us. In Christ, we embrace a future of grace, love, and understanding.

We renounce healthy patterns of communication and behavior that have hindered our relationship. We commit ourselves to love one another with patience, kindness, and respect, choosing to build each other up instead of tearing each other down. With the Holy Spirit as our guide, we will cultivate a home of peace and support.

We renounce selfishness in our marriage. We commit to putting each other's needs above our own, following the example of Christ who selflessly served. We will seek to understand and to honor each other, making sacrifices for one another as an expression of our love.

We renounce doubt and fear regarding our future together. We place our trust in God, who has the power to restore and redeem. We proclaim our faith in His promises, knowing that with Him, all things are possible. We will walk hand in hand, anchored in the hope and love of Christ, confidently facing whatever comes our way.

WIFE'S
thoughts

HUSBAND'S
thoughts

CHRIST CENTERED UNION

WRITTEN BY MARCOS & MELANIE AVILES

Ecclesiastes 4:12 (NIV)
"Be though one may be overpowered, two can defend themselves. A cord of three strands is not quickly broken."

D ear married couples, coming into our marriage there was so much hurt and anger buried down deep within us. There were things that were suppressed and never dealt with which caused us to live out the saying that goes, "hurt people hurt people." Our marriage was a constant battle all the time.

There were times that we didn't even want to be near each other. We had allowed the unhealed parts of our past to become the driving force of our marriage. There was so much unforgiveness, bitterness, rejection, pride, and more hate than anything else. Our fits of anger turned into hurtful things that caused us to tear each other down to the point that one day we sat at our dining room table and began to talk about getting a divorce. We even discussed how we were going to explain it to our daughters. One of the most painful moments of our lives honestly.

The enemy had us right where he wanted us. Staring at divorce, a curse that was in our bloodline because our parents had been divorced. We knew something had to be done. There had to be a way to get things right. We tried whatever we could to get the help we needed, but we didn't see any hope.

All we saw was hopelessness. We knew that there was something missing in our marriage. Yes, we believed in God and were saved, but Jesus wasn't the center of our marriage.

We never fully surrendered to the Lord. We did things our way and never let Him take the reins. It wasn't until one day that we said "enough!" That day we came to our senses and knew that the enemy's plan was for us to destroy each other but God's plan was for us to flourish and thrive together as husband and wife. He says in the word that His plans is to prosper us and not harm us. Divorce would not only harm us, but also hurt our children and our family.

We had to make a choice to not give up. We had to release the pain. We had to release all the offense and unforgiveness. We had to say out of our own mouths, "JESUS WE NEED YOU!" It was right at that moment that the Lord came in and redeemed the time! He restored us, healed us, set us free, and became the satisfaction to our needs. We were staring at the end of our marriage but Jesus came in and turned it around. He gave us hope again. He removed the scales from our eyes. He went into those deep dark places within us and turned on the lights again. Now when we look at each other we look at each other with true love. It was all because of Jesus. The moment we took ourselves out of the way and let Him have control of our marriage is when the fighting ceased and the hurt ended. Jesus saved our marriage and now we can live and tell the world about it!

COUPLES PRAYER:

Heavenly Father, as we journey together, may our hearts remain aligned with Yours. Guide us through the challenges we face and bless our moments of joy. Help us to prioritize prayer, worship, and service in our lives, both individually and as a couple. We pray that our home is filled with Your love, peace, and joy, and that our lives reflect Your light to those around us. Keep us anchored in Your Word, and let our relationship be a testament to Your grace and goodness. In Jesus name, Amen.

REFLECTION:

Identify any challenges you face in establishing or deepening a God-centered aspect in your marriage. What specific steps can you take to address these challenges and grow closer to your partner?Describe your vision for your marriage as a God-centered partnership. What qualities or habits do you wish to cultivate individually and together to align more closely with this vision?

 Take your time with these questions and jot down your thoughts in a journal or share them with your partner for deeper discussion. Consider how this reflection can guide your journey toward a more fulfilling marriage.

DELIVERANCE DECREES

DESTROYING SEEDS OF DISCORD

As Believers we have the authority to speak forth decrees that destroy the seeds of discord. By declaring these words out loud, we align ourselves with the truth of God's Word and invite His deliverance into our marriage.

Decree:

In the name of Jesus, we decree that our marriage shall be a reflection of Christ's love for the Church, rooted in faith, grace, and mutual respect. We recognize that our union is a divine covenant, and we commit to honoring and cherishing each other as partners in this holy relationship.

Renunciations:

We renounce selfishness and the desire to prioritize our own needs above each other. We commit to seeking the best for one another, reflecting the love of Christ in our relationship.

We renounce all forms of bitterness and resentment. We choose to forgive one another as Christ forgave us, allowing grace to flow freely in our marriage.

We renounce dishonesty in all forms, including deceitful communication and hidden grievances. We commit to transparency and trust, building our marriage on honesty and openness.

We renounce any attitudes or actions that foster division between us. We commit to nurturing unity and harmony in our marriage, recognizing that together, we can fulfill God's purpose for our lives.

WIFE'S
thoughts

HUSBAND'S
thoughts

INTENTIONAL SURRENDERANCE

WRITTEN BY DANIEL & CHRISTIE RIOS

Mark 10:9 (NIV)
"Be Therefore, what God has joined together, let no one separate."

Dear married couples, Throughout the eight years we've been married we've faced many hurdles that almost completely broke us. We are called to ministry together, and began working in ministry together on a high level since right after we got married. We were facing so many demonic attacks that were causing so much division in our marriage and family that tormented us for years. We made ministry and the church idols, and had so many people crossing boundaries in our lives that the strongholds were heavy and substantial. Constantly having tumultuous fights, constantly putting everything else before our marriage and family, and having others speak negatively into our lives that it was all starting to fall apart before us.

We were being tormented every night by the open doors that were all over in our lives, and on multiple occasions we almost got divorced. There were times we didn't speak for days, but would do ministry with a smile plastered on our faces because we thought that's what God wanted. However, the enemy was ravaging through our household and we had ill words spoken on every side of us causing us to drift further and further apart until we were riding on fumes.

We were pouring into others constantly and falling apart inwardly, not noticing the religious and controlling spirits that were dominating our lives. But God didn't forget us. After years of this, we experienced a supernatural conviction of the Lord that rose up within each of us at almost the exact same time and the scales started falling off our eyes of what was happening. It was the most united we'd ever been and it surprised both of us, so we decided to press in and see what God needed of us. We intentionally came together and began praying, fasting, seeking wise counsel, and truly listening to the voice of God like never before. We soon went through deliverance and a breaking of all those strongholds, and chose to seek the Lord above all else and a radical change started to happen to us individually and in our marriage, which actually then trailed down to our kids experiencing the blaze of God's fire within them. We set new healthy patterns in place and dove headfirst into God and the Core Group, and we started to see a shift that happened so quickly.

Throughout our whole time in ministry, preaching, praying, prophesying, teaching, and ministering on an individual and congregational level, we thought we were on fire for God. We knew the things of God, but didn't know Him the way He wanted us to know Him. Little did we know what real revival fire felt like until blazed through our marriage and family after we chose to lay our lives and marriage at His feet. Seven years of torment, with the eighth year finding restoration in God. We are a true testimony that nothing is impossible for Him and we can truly say, by the power of the Holy Ghost, we have a delivered marriage.

COUPLES PRAYER:

Lord, we ask that You cover us with Your divine shield. In the name of Jesus, we break any negative words, curses, or judgments spoken over us, whether from others or from ourselves. We declare that these words have no power over our lives, for Your truth and promises reign supreme. Father, we ask for Your wisdom to identify any negative thoughts we may harbor and to replace them with affirmations of Your love and truth. We pray for healing from any hurt caused by negative words in the past. Help us to forgive those who have spoken against us and to let go of any bitterness. Fill our hearts with love, and let our words reflect Your goodness. As we stand together in unity, strengthen our bond and help us to always support and uplift each other. May our relationship be a testament to Your grace and love. In Jesus name, Amen.

REFLECTION:

Reflect on a time when you've witnessed or experienced the impact of negative words on your marriage. Consider how the couple in the book managed to break these negative patterns and what you can learn from their experience. How can you apply this lesson to your own relationships or interactions with others?

DELIVERANCE DECREES

BREAKING NEGATIVE WORDS AND WORD CURSES

As Believers we have the authority to speak forth decrees that break negative words curses off your lives. By declaring these words out loud, we align ourselves with the truth of God's Word and invite His deliverance into our marriage.

Decree:

In the name of Jesus, we decree that we will speak words of affirmation, hope, and encouragement to one another. We will nurture our marriage with kindness, patience, and love, reflecting Your heart towards each other.

Renunciations:

We renounce any curses and negative words spoken over my marriage, whether by others or ourselves. We break every generational curse and claim the healing power of Christ over our marriage. We choose to release all past hurts and embrace a future filled with love, grace, and forgiveness.

We renounce any bitterness or resentment that may have taken root in our hearts. I renounce any harsh words or judgments made against my spouse. Instead, we commit to speak with kindness, understanding, and humility, fostering an environment of love and reconciliation in our marriage.

We renounce any words of destruction, criticism, or condemnation that have hurt us. Instead, we choose to speak life, encouragement, and affirmation into our marriage, acknowledging the strengths and the beauty within our union.

We renounce all doubt and fear that have created division in our marriage. I choose to trust in God's promises and believe in His power to restore and strengthen our marriage. I declare that our love is rooted in faith, and we will speak hope and confidence over our union.

WIFE'S
thoughts

HUSBAND'S
thoughts

HEART SHIFTED TO SALVATION

WRITTEN BY DESMOND & JILL BLUE

1 Peter 4:8 (NIV)

"Above all, love one another deeply, because love covers a multitude of sins"

D

ear married couples, we were married in 2010, a young couple just out of college. We were both believers and raised in Christian homes and desired the Lord to be the center of our lives, however, we struggled to understand how to do that. In 2012 we experienced infidelity and its effects on our marriage lasted for years. Our marriage nearly ended, BUT GOD. The Lord worked on our hearts and forgiveness brought healing into our marriage. However, the hurt and shame remained. We were not intimately walking with the Lord, even while we lived as professing Christians. We struggled for years with constant bickering and yelling.

We had no idea how to love each other "as Christ loved the church" or how to "submit to one another" and it felt like we constantly spoke a different language. In 2018 the Lord began to work on my (Jill's) heart, pulling me deeply into consecration and intimacy with him.

He changed the way I thought, spoke, and acted and it was a huge adjustment for our marriage. In 2021, I went through deliverance and was set free from the spirit of rejection that had affected much of my mind and emotions, for most of my life. As the Lord began to heal and shift my life, Desmond began to see how changed I was.

Watching Jill change was challenging for me (Desmond). I wanted to believe it was true, but I had seen behavior modification in the past and knew how temporary it could be. Up until that point, I had not encountered the love of God in its fullness and I did not know how He could truly change hearts in the way that he can. I often felt irritated by the changes Jill made- like not watching TV or listening to music she once had. I couldn't understand the shift.

I (Jill) prayed often for Desmond that the Lord would work in his heart and life, as he had in mine. The Lord led us both through a great deal of continued healing and deliverance. At a marriage retreat in 2022, Desmond was set free from the spirit of shame and he encountered the love of God like never before. I (Desmond) could finally see that God truly cares and there is nothing that separates me from His love.

This knowledge removed guilt and shame and showed me He has always been with me. His love began to teach me how to live in freedom and victory.
Now that our eyes are free from the lenses of guilt, shame, and rejection, we can see one another clearly through the love of God. He has taught us how to love, lead, and submit in our marriage and individually with Him. This has healed our marriage and grown it in ways we never could have imagined, or produced on our own. We give all glory to God, GREAT things He has done!

COUPLES PRAYER:

Heavenly Father, we lift up our spouse into Your loving hands. We pray for their heart to be open to Your Word and for them to come to know the depth of Your love and salvation. Remove any barriers that stand in the way of their faith. We ask for Your Holy Spirit to guide our conversations and interactions. Help us to speak words of life and encouragement, avoiding criticism and judgment. May our relationship be a reflection of Your love, drawing us closer to each other and to You. Lord, renew our hearts and minds. Help us to support one another in our walk with you. May we be patient and kind, always trusting in Your perfect plan for our lives and our marriage. In Jesus name, Amen.

REFLECTION:

How do you relate to the themes of shame and guilt in your own life? Are there specific situations or experiences that have left you feeling burdened by these emotions? How has your spouse encouraged you to change? Take your time to meditate on these questions, and feel free to journal your thoughts.

Allow this reflection to deepen your understanding of the power of now allowing shame and guilt to keep you in bondage.

DELIVERANCE DECREES

BREAKING THE SPIRIT OF GUILT AND SAME

As Believers we have the authority to speak forth decrees that break the power of guilt and shame in our lives. By declaring these words out loud, we align ourselves with the truth of God's Word and invite His deliverance into our marriage.

Decree:

In the name of Jesus, I break every stronghold of guilt and shame that has been established in our marriage. I declare that we are free from judgment and accusation, both from within ourselves and from external sources. We embrace a spirit of grace, acceptance, and unconditional love for one another, in alignment with Ephesians 4:32, which commands us to forgive one another as Christ forgave us.

Renunciations:

We renounce the guilt that hinders our relationship with you and each other. We refuse to carry the burdens of past mistakes, knowing that Christ has paid the price for our sins.

We renounce the shame that distorts my self-image and my view of my spouse. I reject the lies that tell us that we're unworthy of love and acceptance.

We renounce the fear that keeps us from vulnerability and intimacy in our marriage. We refuse to let fear dictate our actions or our love.

We renounce any bitterness or resentment we hold in our heart towards each other. We will not allow past grievances to affect our future.

WIFE'S
thoughts

HUSBAND'S
thoughts

VICTORY IN UNITY

WRITTEN BY JOSH & CIARA GRIFFIN

Ephesians 4:3 (NIV)
"Make every effort to keep yourselves united in the Spirit, binding yourselves together with peace."

D ear married couples, we met on Christianmingle.com so right away, we KNEW we both desired a spouse with a mutual savior named Jesus. I would love to say that we walked by the Spirit of God from the moment we met, but rather, we were still walking by several other spirits apart of satan's army.

Our relationship was founded on the morals and values of the Bible, but quickly we introduced each other to our own lusts, perversion, idolatry, pornography addiction, drug addiction, pride, depression, anxiety, and torment. Serving alongside each other in ministry bound with all of these things, our spirits always craved MORE. Despite the battles, we pressed for the will of Almighty God in what we did, and where we went. We followed His leading, moving place to place, each rendering a new and needed season of healing, growing, and more hunger.

When we learned of deliverance from the demonic, it changed everything. We both received our freedom in Christ and broke through mold of where the devil wanted us to be kept. We emerged forward in victory TOGETHER, as a double threat to the enemy's camp. We are now thriving, walking by the Holy Spirit of God, training up 3 children who we have broken the bloodline for, and ministering full time as a part of the Core Group. We glorify God for every single mountain and valley. It is by the very hand of God that we received our miracle of a Biblical marriage. We will never be the same!

COUPLES PRAYER:

Father, we ask that as we face challenges together, grant us the wisdom to see things from each other's perspective. Help us to support one another, lift each other up, and celebrate our victories together. Remind us that together, we are stronger, and with You by our side, there is nothing we cannot overcome. We pray for the victory of harmony in our home, peace in our hearts, and joy in our lives. May our love reflect Your love, and may we be witnesses to Your greatness through our partnership. In moments of struggle, remind us of Your promises and the strength we find in You. May we always seek to honor one another and cherish the bond we share.

REFLECTION:

Their testimony highlights a significant transformation through deliverance and healing. What does "freedom in Christ" mean to you, personally? Can you identify moments in your life where you felt stuck or bound, and how might you seek freedom from those areas?

They discussed breaking the bloodline for their children. What legacy do you seek to create for your family? How can you actively break negative cycles and instill positive values in those around you?

DELIVERANCE DECREES

BREAKING THE SPIRIT OF PRIDE

As Believers we have the authority to speak forth decrees that break the power of pride in our lives. By declaring these words out loud, we align ourselves with the truth of God's Word and invite His deliverance into our marriage.

Decree:

In the name of Jesus, we decree that any past hurts and grievances fueled by pride are forgiven and released. We speak healing into our marriage, and we declare that we will move forward in unity and love.

Renunciations:

We renounce the comparison of our marriage to others, which fosters discontent and breeds pride. We commit to appreciating the unique journey we share in our marriage, celebrating our individual strengths and the work God is doing in us together.

We renounce the spirit of judgment and criticism that leads us to focus on our spouse's flaws while ignoring our own. We commit to offering grace and encouragement, choosing to build each other up with loving words and actions, and to foster a spirit of unity and understanding.

We renounce the pursuit of our own selfish ambitions and desires that prioritize our needs above each other. We commit to placing my each others needs and feelings before our own, seeking to serve each other with love and respect as modeled by Christ.

We renounce any hard-heartedness and unwillingness to forgive that creates barriers between each other. We commit to embracing a spirit of humility, offering forgiveness freely as we have been forgiven, and fostering an environment of open communication and reconciliation in our marriage.

WIFE'S
thoughts

HUSBAND'S
thoughts

OUR

Notes

OUR
Notes

OUR
Notes

OUR Notes

OUR
Notes

OUR
Notes

OUR

Notes

OUR
Notes

OUR
Notes

OUR
Notes

OUR Notes

OUR
Notes

OUR
Notes

OUR
Notes

OUR
Notes

OUR Notes

OUR

Notes

OUR
Notes

OUR
Notes

OUR
Notes

OUR Notes

OUR Notes

OUR
Notes

Made in the USA
Middletown, DE
22 August 2024

59054117R00044